Daniel McGinn

Drowning the Boy

SurVision Books

First published in 2022 by
SurVision Books
Dublin, Ireland
Reggio di Calabria, Italy
www.survisionmagazine.com

Copyright © Daniel McGinn, 2022
Cover image © Michael McGinn, 2022
Design © SurVision Books, 2022

ISBN: 978-1-912963-36-2

This book is in copyright. No part of this publication may be reproduced, stored in a retrieval system, or transmitted in any form or by any means without the prior permission in writing from the publisher.

Acknowledgments

Grateful acknowledgment is made to the editors of the following, in which some of these poems, or versions of them, originally appeared:

Amateur Surrealist Descending a Staircase (Laguna Poets Series #132): "Silent Flick"

Lummox Magazine: "Every Shell on This Beach Is Empty"

SurVision: "He Goes Walking after Midnight"

CONTENTS

Pen and Ink	7
The Gods	8
His Body Curls into Sleep	9
The Wind Is Moving	10
Lady in Velvet	11
Silent Flick	12
Ghost Dog	13
Drowning the Boy	14
He Wakes Up	15
Survivor	16
Tap-Tap Therapy	17
He Goes Walking after Midnight	18
The Crossroad at Noe Valley	19
She Asked for Sex Oil	20
California Mouth	21
She Said Close My Eyes	22
Firebug	23
Sword Swallower	24
Mercury Mouth	25
Greetings from the Carpet Store	26
Every Shell on This Beach Is Empty	27
The Sun Sets over His Back Yard	28
He Was a Pool of Molten Steel	29
Forgetting	30
A Crust of Bread under the Table	31
Death by Chocolate	32
The Boy	33

For Padraic Cohee
who housed our poems in chapbooks
and opened many doors

Pen and Ink

He draws a line between bird and fish
That's where he lives
His left hand draws a face and smears the ink
A face has lines
He sees you read his face
and writes the word sorry on his forehead
He didn't mean to do it
He smears that word too
He swallows the word sin like a wafer
His mouth snaps shut like a clam
He draws himself a closet and shuts the door
He is a friend to the dark and the quiet
He's a self-made man
A man made of sticks
He sketches a boat
He draws V birds in a paper sky
Ahoy he says The water glares at him
Ahoy he says Fish duck their heads
The gulls begin to cry

The Gods

It's snowing The boy doesn't know he's walking
on a lake A speck of dust across a blank canvas
A blue swirl from a fan-tail brush wets the frozen
white where the child used to be

Half-lit room with beige walls Blonde woman
A gray chair in the corner No shadows
Her eyes are wet and swollen She's not finished
You can't tell her when she is finished Don't

In a field of flies a man pretends he's in a war
movie He shoots his rake like a gun He runs
around like a hero kicking watermelons
rotting in the summer sun He boots the bloated
bodies of the stinking dead

His Body Curls into Sleep

the white door meets him
he enters the dream

the door must be a woman
the door is warm as milk

sleep is a brass key turning
between tongue and teeth

sometimes the door is open
sometimes the door is closed

his thoughts at the end of the day
were hard and he felt like crying

he was trained not to
real men cry with fists

a spinning fan is pointing
out the window it blows

stale thoughts into the yard
the lawn outside his window

is the dead straw stubble
of what once was grass

The Wind Is Moving

the lily white
white lily stops
the wind

cups the breath
in her flower face

her flower face
the wind is moving
moving wind

Lady in Velvet

trapped in a closed fist
a remnant of light
eludes his grasp
like air from a feather pillow

she arrives somewhere
between sleep and dream
wearing that dress
made of velvet and blood

he is hushed
like a silent movie
in a dark theater
everyone is watching

in the same room
in the same bed
nothing is the same
and always

breathing is ocean
until waves stop breaking
his legs hold back
their own tiny earthquakes

always arriving
always leaving
the exhale and inhale
the same stale air

Silent Flick

eyes beautiful wet
adjust to the light
silhouettes and shadows
rise from their chairs

adjust to the light
a series of events
rise from their chairs
the last thing he sees

a series of events
pass in slow motion
the last thing he sees
falling like snow

passing in slow motion
clouds appear
falling like snow
everything white

clouds appear
silhouettes and shadows
everything white
eyes beautiful wet

Ghost Dog

He sees a dog in the corner of his eye
float by faint as a thumbprint or a shadow
pressed in the air When he turns off the lights
darkness leans on him like a weighted blanket
He dreams black coffee blackbirds blackberries
never pencil sketches always pen and ink
The sun goes down his shadow goes with it
He gets lonely You were always ice cold
A half moon hidden beneath a gray hand
A growl of wind at the end of a tunnel
A white mop dropped in a dog food bowl
You were the one you taught him not to cry
to say excuse me to let you go first
The house gets chilly when the ghost dog barks

Drowning the Boy

The boy slept with his head buried in a feather pillow
The sun burned a circle on the child's back
The shadow of god swooped down like a crow
Talons dug into his shoulders
pinning the boy to the bottom of the boat

A black beak opened and closed on a neck bone
savoring it as if it were a good seed
pressing hard enough to warn the boy not to raise his head
The boy didn't believe in gods he was conflicted about birds
He was having a hard time breathing

The bed began to rock like an autistic chair
The bed was a boat on a body of water
The child felt the water begin
Moist against his body
Cold again his hip bones

The boy wasn't crying He didn't wet the bed
He was trapped in a boat The boat was wet
He couldn't lift his face He no longer had a face
His head was buried in a bag of feathers
The crow was his father This boy had sinned

He Wakes Up

to the sound of a dog barking parents slurring their words He can't see anything lying there in the dark clutching the top of a blanket Their voices are hushed Their emotions are loud like the football player behind the rose bushes who punched him once and called him a pussy in a voice so low it was almost a whisper The boy already knew he was a pussy He closed his eyes lowered his head and started punching the air He felt helpless straining to hear what his father was saying His mother was yelling Her words like the boy's punches The boy's father walked away quietly shutting the door behind him just like he did every day for the rest of the boy's life

Survivor

Letters stumbled out of your mouth on crippled legs
when you called the boy by his childhood name
The boy's name was bigger than the boy
He had to look up to see you He was that small

When you spoke to him windows shattered
Bits of glass glinted the air You stretched a ribbon
of caution tape across his mouth It sagged slightly
like Miss America's sash You hung a realtor's lock
on his doorknob Spiders made a home inside the lock

That small house was his playhouse
where the boy's secret name sucked blood
from the breasts of frightened insects

Tap-Tap Therapy

She holds two fingers against her thumb
like a sock puppet stabbing the air

The boy is distracted by her fingers
tap-tap tapping out a distress signal and he is fascinated

by her hand
floating inches above the table nails pointed down

pecking like a pigeon on a fast food wrapper
Once I started writing about it

I couldn't stop remembering it she says
and then I couldn't stop crying

Her hands are deliberate like a crow's beak
plucking meat from a dead rat

The boy finds the look on her face disturbing
You should be tapping too

she says it helps relieve stress Should I be
tapping the table He asks

No she says tap on yourself Then she shows him
tap tapping her arms her thighs and her face

He knows right away that he shouldn't try this
He doesn't want to start slapping himself again

He Goes Walking after Midnight

Before the sun caused cars to spill into the streets
he was alone listening to his boot heels echo

against the sidewalk under streetlights spaced
like traffic cones throwing spotlights at silence

It's never silent not really The air around here
pricks a boy's skin like pine needles

When he passes under telephone wires
their hum enters him

He lives close to sea level but not close enough
to see waves break If he listens intently he hears

sirens howl like wolves in the distance
Sometimes they travel in packs

The Crossroad at Noe Valley

The sun has risen No one lingers under the streetlight
This used to be a four-way intersection
in the shape of a crucifix One side of the road has fallen
down the hill Carefully squeeze between the houses up ahead
Don't stop where the street narrows even when buildings start
to lean in on you Keep to the right Avoid the road
that goes onto the sidewalk and into the house on the left
Don't go into the house on the left there's a bloodstain
in the sky right above the place Pay no attention to the ghost
of a man under the red light pulsing from that woman's window
He's not an apparition but made of flesh and blood
like a Jehovah's Witness fishing for the broken the widowed
the sheep He's no Moses The man is a wolf He can smell it on you
He craves attention If you give him some you will find him
hanging around your front door If you lived around here
you'd learn soon enough to look right through him
as if he wasn't there and soon enough he isn't

She Asked for Sex Oil

All he had was Crisco
She put it on herself

Her skin was butter
He loves butter

They begin to mix it up
the bed smells like French fries

He goes to the refrigerator
to get the ketchup

No
she says don't

California Mouth

her mouth is an ocean with a bottle at its shore
her mouth is an ocean that matches her hairdo

it crashes into one ear and breaks out the other
her mouth is an ocean surrounded by sand

grains that cling to her white picket teeth
her mouth is an ocean where birds lose their way

her humor? her humor is dry
her mouth is an ocean where sharks fish for seals

in a creaky blue basement below the lump in her throat
her mouth is an ocean

her lipstick is gleaming
the sun bounces beachballs on her silver tooth

She Said Close My Eyes

Then she stared at him He reached across the table
and touched each eyebrow softly at first
so as not to startle them

The one on the right responded like a caterpillar
if you've ever touched one you know what I mean
the way its back arches lets you know

there is muscle enough to propel a body forward
He lingered there for maybe a minute perhaps a mile
time moves quickly when a man grows older

He rested his finger on her eyelid
The caterpillar shivered just a bit but clung to her
like a milkwood stem

He pinched each lash
and pulled down the shades
She never said nothing

He was expecting butterflies
She went blank like a page
and he had no words

Firebug

Sleeping with her is like sleeping with a witch's broom
—Richard Brautigan

Sleeping with him is like riding a rhinoceros She holds tight to the devil's horn He misbehaves like an arsonist burning fingertips starting a sequence of tiny fires making light of everything She infests him like a swarm of ants bumps against him like a pinball machine clatters his bones like a jar of nails Pushing him down she leans in toward his ear and whispers death is a good word He's watching in the mirror as he reaches between her legs It's damp as a sea urchin It stings his skin as water surges out of her One of them is sobbing now Maybe it's an apparition tapping on her door or just the multiplicity of raindrops leaping from the roof and flooding all the gutters

Sword Swallower

She could work miracles with eucalyptus lozenges
and a well-timed sneeze
When she fell for the fly he wasn't surprised
having seen the freaks she'd slept with

He'd also seen the Cronenberg film
and expected the fly to be smudged
and greased like a dumpster diver
fascinated by feces That wasn't the case

He was astonished at how dapper a fly could dress
He was a high-energy fellow
who couldn't sit still for long but when he stopped
he liked fold and unfold limbs at right angles
His appendages formed triangles

I could see she liked him He had pizazz
He didn't look at her when he talked
He looked through her and all around her
She was mesmerized when he spoke
She couldn't stop staring at the slit that split
the tip of his tongue in two

Mercury Mouth

There is an ocean where her voice has been

See the empty bottles strewn along the shore

He scavenges for messages the water washed away

He sits there for hours waiting for the next wave

Crows pepper themselves into flocks of gulls

The nurse arrives wearing her white smock

She opens his arms and starts bleeding him

His tributaries empty into her presence

Greetings from the Carpet Store

She would love this place They have free samples
that smell like chemicals and airplane glue If drugs
had fur you could pet them and find them in the poolside
carpet selection that he fell in love with You can't help
but huff while standing in the aisle Anyone can take
as much as they want for free That made him think of her
Remember when they went swimming at her parent's house
Holding their breath underwater sounded like the music
they'd been listening to Remember her Dad lighting
the barbeque Hamburgers bleeding grease that flared
like little volcanoes over glowing coals He couldn't eat a thing
but those burger patties helped him understand Dead meat
is just a part of life like warped air they mashed between
their faces when they kissed He remembers her warm skin
under the cold that radiated from her swimsuit on that hot
summer day They were dripping wet but chlorine smelled
like expensive perfume on her

Every Shell on This Beach Is Empty

So many things
have gone to pieces
His poor heart beats
in a stitched cage

She can run to him
She can pull away
He can learn to stop
and actually listen

His mouth says
baby won't you
please stop crying
His heart says

go on
give me an ocean

The Sun Sets over His Back Yard

The patio roof aches
like an old man's back
The broke-down slats
give up symmetry

They plant succulents
in a dry fountain
water weeds
in what's left of grass

Leaves fall
They get no fruit
No lilies spring
from the flower bed

He asks the living
to bury the dead

He Was a Pool of Molten Steel

curled into her lap they harden together in silence
there was no time back then when they were not glowing

The air conditioner was in a carload of flowers
Her face was too young for her blazing eyes

They brought boxes of holidays down from the rafters
as if there was a way to go back home

Side by side they bury their parents

See the water slipping under the bridge
their reflections floating on funhouse ripples

that sink like a boat when the sea catches fire
the sun drops like a curtain into the grumbling dark

Forgetting

confused sometimes not sure he remembers
what he read also what he said he waits
in line for gas He gets to the pump
He doesn't have a card he doesn't know
when he lost it Friends started dying
he has mixed feelings Sometimes he grieves
sometimes he forgets What he had to say
doesn't interest him If he doesn't write it down
part of him is sad He remembers sadness
how it comes and goes how it grows up
and moves into a place of its own

Yesterday he made eggs for himself and left
the burner on All those little flames
burning for no good reason What a waste
of energy His wife lets him know what he did
and he says I'm sorry

A Crust of Bread under the Table

hard dry
impossible to swallow

an uneaten meal shivers
under a smothering of mold

The swollen sky
perched above a bloated lake

stops his thoughts
and pinches every nerve

night blooming jasmine
breeze into his lungs

His eyes water
The faucet drips

in the room next door
He won't sleep

He's not hungry
He won't eat

Death by Chocolate

He wanted to talk about the future
He took Death out for a cup of coffee

I assume you like yours black
He said to Death

Death said no
I'll have a white chocolate mocha

with little marshmallows
floating on the top

Is that for here
the barista asked

Death said no
He'll take it to go

The Boy

is standing onstage with his back to the audience
A vaudevillian in top hat and tails enters from center stage
A pie tin brimming with shaving cream perched on his fingers
He crosses the stage with Groucho steps and slams the tin
into the boy's face The audience laughs The boy slowly turns
to the audience revealing that the pie tin has become a mask
a tin replica of a divided face with one side laughing
and the other crying The vaudevillian slowly peels the mask
from the boy's face revealing another mask underneath it
then another mask and another The audience sits in silence
as one by one masks drop below the footlights
The vaudevillian spreads his fingers wide like a deck of cards
he passes his hand in front of the child's face In a flash of light
the boy disappears The audience gasps and applauds
The boy never hears it He's trapped the shadow of an old man
standing in a boat squinting at the sun wondering
where everybody went Ahoy he says Ahoy!

Selected Poetry Titles Published by SurVision Books

Seeds of Gravity: An Anthology of Contemporary Surrealist Poetry from Ireland
Edited by Anatoly Kudryavitsky
ISBN 978-1-912963-18-8

Invasion: An Anthology of Ukrainian Poetry about the War
Edited by Tony Kitt
ISBN 978-1-912963-32-4

Noelle Kocot. *Humanity*
(New Poetics: USA)
ISBN 978-1-9995903-0-7

Marc Vincenz. *Einstein Fledermaus*
(New Poetics: USA)
ISBN 978-1-912963-20-1

Helen Ivory. *Maps of the Abandoned City*
(New Poetics: England)
ISBN 978-1-912963-04-1

Tony Kitt. *The Magic Phlute*
(New Poetics: Ireland)
ISBN 978-1-912963-08-9

Clayre Benzadón. *Liminal Zenith*
(New Poetics: USA)
ISBN 978-1-912963-11-9

Thomas Townsley. *Tangent of Ardency*
(New Poetics: USA)
ISBN 978-1-912963-15-7

Anton Yakovlev. *Chronos Dines Alone*
(Winner of James Tate Poetry Prize 2018)
ISBN 978-1-912963-01-0

Mikko Harvey & Jake Bauer. *Idaho Falls*
(Winner of James Tate Poetry Prize 2018)
ISBN 978-1-912963-02-7

John Bradley. *Spontaneous Mummification*
(Winner of James Tate Poetry Prize 2019)
ISBN 978-1-912963-13-3

John Thomas Allen. *Rolling in the Third Eye*
(Winner of James Tate Poetry Prize 2019)
ISBN 978-1-912963-15-7

Gary Glauber. *The Covalence of Equanimity*
(Winner of James Tate Poetry Prize 2019)
ISBN 978-1-912963-12-6

Charles Kell. *Pierre Mask*
(Winner of James Tate Poetry Prize 2019)
ISBN 978-1-912963-19-5

John Riccio. *Eye, Romanov*
(Winner of James Tate Poetry Prize 2020)
ISBN 978-1-912963-24-9

Kurt Luchs. *The Sound of One Hand Slapping*
(Winner of James Tate Poetry Prize 2021)
ISBN 978-1-912963-33-1

Philip Venzke. *Chant to Save the World*
(Winner of James Tate Poetry Prize 2021)
ISBN 978-1-912963-35-5

Charles Borkhuis. *Spontaneous Combustion*
(Winner of James Tate Poetry Prize 2021)
ISBN 978-1-912963-30-0

Ciaran O'Driscoll. *Angel Hour*
ISBN 978-1-912963-27-0

Tim Murphy. *Mouth of Shadows*
ISBN 978-1-912963-29-4

George Kalamaras. *That Moment of Wept*
ISBN 978-1-9995903-7-6

George Kalamaras. *Through the Silk-Heavy Rains*
ISBN 978-1-912963-28-7

Order our books from http://survisionmagazine.com/bookshop.htm

www.ingramcontent.com/pod-product-compliance
Lightning Source LLC
Chambersburg PA
CBHW071314060426
42444CB00035B/2616